P   s

Spe   arts

WORDS OF

Challenge

AND

Hope

theWORD
among us®
Press

Published by The Word Among Us Press
7115 Guilford Road
Frederick, Maryland 21704
www.wau.org

17 16 15 14 13   2 3 4 5 6

ISBN: 978-1-59325-247-2
eISBN: 978-1-59325-453-7

Cover design by David Crosson and Andrea Rivas
Cover photo: Getty Images
Inside photo: Catholic News Service

Made and printed in the United States of America
Library of Congress Control Number: 2013945718

CONTENTS

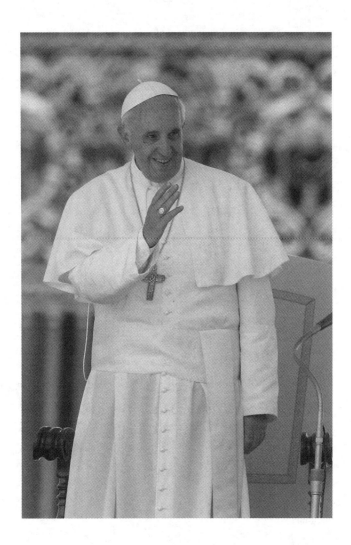

INTRODUCTION

Reflecting on the words of any pope helps us to grow in our faith—after all, he is our shepherd, the one who calls us on as one body in Christ. But Pope Francis, in particular, has a special gift of saying just what we need to hear. His words, as described by the subtitle of this book, are both challenging and filled with hope. Challenging, because he calls us out of our individual comfort zones to be missionaries of God's love in a world that desperately needs to hear the Good News. And hopeful, because he continually points us to the love and mercy of God, a Father "who always waits for us, even when we have left him behind!"

These short excerpts are taken from Pope Francis' addresses and homilies since his election and reflect the themes that we can expect to hear again and again during his pontificate. Among them are the mercy of God, the scandal of poverty, the need to "come out of ourselves" to evangelize, the call to unity in the Church, and the challenge to become true disciples of Jesus and not "part-time

Christians." Francis has become known for his simple and down-to-earth way of communicating these truths, and his genius is his ability to show us how our faith should be lived out in real and tangible ways. And while he does not shrink from telling us the hard things we need to hear, he also assures us that our God is a God of mercy who never tires of forgiving us.

We hope you will be blessed by Pope Francis' words, as we were as we compiled this book. With the universal Church, we pray that Pope Francis' pontificate will continue to inspire and strengthen each one of us so that we may draw closer to the Lord and heed his call to "go . . . and make disciples of all nations" (Matthew 28:19).

The Word Among Us Press

CHAPTER

1

THE TENDER
LOVE OF GOD

God's Name Is Love

Let us recognize that God is not something vague; our God is not a God "spray"; he is tangible; he is not abstract but has a name: "God is love." His is not a sentimental, emotional kind of love but the love of the Father who is the origin of all life, the love of the Son who dies on the cross and is raised, the love of the Spirit who renews human beings and the world. Thinking that God is love does us so much good, because it teaches us to love, to give ourselves to others as Jesus gave himself to us and walks with us. Jesus walks beside us on the road through life.

The Cascade of Tenderness

As when a mother takes her child upon her knee and caresses him or her: so the Lord will do and does with us. This is the cascade of tenderness which gives us much consolation. "As one whom his mother comforts, so I will comfort you" (Isaiah 66:13). Every Christian, and especially you and I, is called to be a bearer of this message of hope that gives serenity and joy: God's consolation, his tenderness towards all. But if we first experience the joy of being consoled by him, of being loved by him, then we can bring that joy to others. This is important if our mission is to be fruitful: to feel God's consolation and to pass it on to others!

Faith in God's Tangible Love

Our culture has lost its sense of God's tangible presence and activity in our world. We think that God is to be found in the beyond, on another level of reality, far removed from our everyday relationships. But if this were the case, if God could not act in the world, his love would not be truly powerful, truly real, and thus not even true, a love capable of delivering the bliss that it promises. It would make no difference at all whether we believed in him or not. Christians, on the contrary, profess their faith in God's tangible and powerful love which really does act in history and determines its final destiny: a love that can be encountered, a love fully revealed in Christ's passion, death, and resurrection.

We Are Not a Number to God

For God, we are not numbers; we are important; indeed, we are the most important thing to him. Even if we are sinners, we are what is closest to his heart.

God Takes the First Step

God does not wait for us to go to him, but it is he who moves toward us, without calculation, without quantification. That is what God is like. He always takes the first step; he comes toward us.

Like a Shepherd

God thinks like the Samaritan who did not pass by the unfortunate man, pitying him or looking at him from the other side of the road, but helped him without asking for anything in return; without asking whether he was a Jew, a pagan, or a Samaritan, whether he was rich or poor; he asked for nothing. He went to help him. God is like this. God thinks like the shepherd who lays down his life in order to defend and save his sheep.

God's Love: Stronger Than Death

We, too, like the women who were Jesus' disciples, who went to the tomb and found it empty, may wonder what this event means (cf. Luke 24:4). What does it mean that Jesus is risen? It means that the love of God is stronger than evil and death itself; it means that the love of God can transform our lives and let those desert places in our hearts bloom. The love of God can do this!

God Is Patient with Us

God is not impatient like us, who often want everything all at once, even in our dealings with other people. God is patient with us because he loves us, and those who love are able to understand, to hope, to inspire confidence; they do not give up, they do not burn bridges, they are able to forgive. Let us remember this in our lives as Christians: God always waits for us, even when we have left him behind! He is never far from us, and if we return to him, he is ready to embrace us.

A Completely Reliable Love

Christ's death discloses the utter reliability of God's love above all in the light of his resurrection. As the Risen One, Christ is the trustworthy witness, deserving of faith (cf. Revelation 1:5; Hebrews 2:17), and a solid support for our faith. "If Christ has not been raised, your faith is futile," says St. Paul (1 Corinthians 15:17). Had the Father's love not caused Jesus to rise from the dead, had it not been able to restore his body to life, then it would not be a completely reliable love, capable of illuminating also the gloom of death.

He Seeks Us

Adam, after his sin, experiences shame; he feels naked, he senses the weight of what he has done, and yet God does not abandon him. If that moment of sin marks the beginning of his exile from God, there is already a promise of return, a possibility of return. God immediately asks, "Adam, where are you?" He seeks him out.

God Never Forgets Us

God treats us as children; he understands us, he forgives us, he embraces us, he loves us even when we err. In the Old Testament, the prophet Isaiah was already affirming that even if a mother could forget her child, God never forgets us at any moment (cf. 49:15). And this is beautiful!

Bring God's Consolation to Others

The Lord is a Father, and he says that he will be for us like a mother with her baby, with a mother's tenderness. Do not be afraid of the consolations of the Lord. Isaiah's invitation must resound in our hearts: "Comfort, comfort my people" (40:1), and this must lead to mission. We must find the Lord who consoles us and go to console the people of God. This is the mission. People today certainly need words, but most of all they need us to bear witness to the mercy and tenderness of the Lord, which warms the heart, rekindles hope, and attracts people towards the good. What a joy it is to bring God's consolation to others!

Encountering Jesus

Reading about Faith Is Not Enough

When we seek [Jesus], we discover that he is waiting to welcome us, to offer us his love. And this fills your heart with such wonder that you can hardly believe it, and this is how your faith grows—through encounter with a Person, through encounter with the Lord. Some people will say, "No, I prefer to read about faith in books!" It is important to read about faith, but look, on its own, this is not enough! What is important is our encounter with Jesus, our encounter with him, and this is what gives you faith, because he is the One who gives it to you!

Jesus' Voice Is Unique

The mystery of [Jesus'] voice is evocative. Only think that from our mother's womb, we learn to recognize her voice and that of our father; it is from the tone of a voice that we perceive love or contempt, affection or coldness. Jesus' voice is unique! If we learn to distinguish it, he guides us on the path of life, a path that goes beyond even the abyss of death.

Welcome Jesus as a Friend

Let the Risen Jesus enter your life; welcome him as a friend, with trust: he is life! If up till now you have kept him at a distance, step forward. He will receive you with open arms. If you have been indifferent, take a risk; you won't be disappointed. If following him seems difficult, don't be afraid; trust him, be confident that he is close to you. He is with you, and he will give you the peace you are looking for and the strength to live as he would have you do.

Why the Cross?

Why the cross? Because Jesus takes upon himself the evil, the filth, the sin of the world, including the sin of all of us, and he cleanses it: he cleanses it with his blood, with the mercy and the love of God. Let us look around: how many wounds are inflicted upon humanity by evil! Wars, violence, economic conflicts that hit the weakest; greed for money that you can't take with you and have to leave. When we were small, our grandmother used to say, "A shroud has no pocket." Love of power, corruption, divisions, crimes against human life and against creation! And—as each one of us knows and is aware—our personal sins: our failures in love and respect toward God, toward our neighbor, and toward the whole of creation. Jesus on the cross feels the whole weight of the evil, and with the force of God's love he conquers it; he defeats it with his resurrection. This is the good that Jesus does for us on the throne of the cross. Christ's cross embraced with love never leads to sadness but to joy, to the joy of having been saved and of doing a little of what he did on the day of his death.

He Gave Himself Up "for Me"

Jesus gave himself up to death voluntarily in order to reciprocate the love of God the Father, in perfect union with his will, to demonstrate his love for us. On the cross Jesus "loved me and gave himself for me" (Galatians 2:20). Each one of us can say: "He loved me and gave himself for me." Each one can say this "for me."

We Are His Dwelling Place

Jesus lived the daily reality of the most ordinary people: he was moved as he faced the crowd that seemed like a flock without a shepherd; he wept before the sorrow that Martha and Mary felt at the death of their brother, Lazarus; he called a publican to be his disciple; he also suffered betrayal by a friend. In him God has given us the certitude that he is with us, he is among us. "Foxes," he, Jesus, said, "have holes, and birds of the air have nests, but the Son of man has nowhere to lay his head" (Matthew 8:20). Jesus has no house, because his house is the people; it is we who are his dwelling place; his mission is to open God's doors to all, to be the presence of God's love.

Jesus Trusts in His Heavenly Father

The Gospel presents to us the account of the miracle of the multiplication of the loaves (Luke 9:11-17). I would like to reflect on one aspect of it that never fails to impress me and [that] makes me think. We are on the shore of the Sea of Galilee; daylight is fading. Jesus is concerned for the people who have spent so many hours with him: there are thousands of them and they are hungry. What should he do? The disciples also pose the problem and tell Jesus, "Send the crowd away," so that they can go and find provisions in the villages close by. . . .

Jesus' outlook is very different; it is dictated by his union with the Father and his compassion for the people, that mercifulness of Jesus for us all. Jesus senses our problems, he senses our weaknesses, he senses our needs. Looking at those five loaves, Jesus thinks: this is Providence! From this small amount, God can make it suffice for everyone. Jesus trusts in the heavenly Father without reserve; he knows that for him everything is possible.

What Is "the" Truth?

We are living in an age in which people are rather skeptical of truth. Benedict XVI has frequently spoken of relativism, that is, of the tendency to consider nothing definitive and to think that truth comes from consensus or from something we like. The question arises: does "the" truth really exist? What is "the" truth? Can we know it? Can we find it? Here springs to my mind the question of Pontius Pilate, the Roman procurator, when Jesus reveals to him the deep meaning of his mission: "What is truth?" (John 18:37, 38). Pilate cannot understand that "the" Truth is standing in front of him; he cannot see in Jesus the face of the truth that is the face of God. And yet Jesus is exactly this: the Truth that, in the fullness of time, "became flesh" and came to dwell among us so that we might know it (cf. John 1:1, 14). The truth is not grasped as a thing; the truth is encountered. It is not a possession; it is an encounter with a Person.

Christ Is Our Roped Guide

The ascension of Jesus into heaven acquaints us with this deeply consoling reality on our journey: in Christ, true God and true man, our humanity was taken to God. Christ opened the path to us. He is like a roped guide climbing a mountain who, on reaching the summit, pulls us up to him and leads us to God. If we entrust our lives to him, if we let ourselves be guided by him, we are certain to be in safe hands, in the hands of our Savior, of our Advocate.

Present in Every Space and Time

The Ascension does not point to Jesus' absence, but tells us that he is alive in our midst in a new way. He is no longer in a specific place in the world as he was before the Ascension. He is now in the lordship of God, present in every space and time, close to each one of us. In our lives we are never alone: we have this Advocate who awaits us, who defends us. We are never alone: the Crucified and Risen Lord guides us. We have with us a multitude of brothers and sisters who, in silence and concealment, in their family life and at work, in their problems and hardships, in their joys and hopes, live faith daily and together with us bring the world the lordship of God's love, in the Risen Jesus Christ, ascended into heaven, our own Advocate who pleads for us.

The Heart of Jesus: Not Just a Symbol

Popular piety highly values symbols, and the heart of Jesus is the ultimate symbol of God's mercy. But it is not an imaginary symbol; it is a real symbol which represents the center, the source from which salvation flowed for all of humanity.

In the Gospels we find various references to the heart of Jesus. For example, there is a passage in which Christ himself says, "Come to me, all who labor and are heavy laden, and I will give you rest. Take my yoke upon you, and learn from me; for I am gentle and lowly in heart" (Matthew 11:28-29). Then there is the key account of Christ's death according to John. Indeed, this Evangelist bears witness to what he saw on Calvary; that is, when Jesus was already dead, a soldier pierced his side with a spear and blood and water came out of the wound (cf. John 19:33-34). In that apparently coincidental sign, John recognizes the fulfillment of the prophecies: from the heart of Jesus, the Lamb sacrificed on the cross, flow forgiveness and life for all people.

He Makes Himself a Gift

This evening [Solemnity of Corpus Christi], once again, the Lord distributes for us the bread that is his Body; he makes himself a gift, and we, too, experience "God's solidarity" with man, a solidarity that is never depleted, a solidarity that never ceases to amaze us. God makes himself close to us; in the sacrifice of the cross, he humbles himself, entering the darkness of death to give us his life, which overcomes evil, selfishness, and death. Jesus, this evening too, gives himself to us in the Eucharist, shares in our journey; indeed, he makes himself food, the true food which sustains our life also in moments when the road becomes hard going and obstacles slow our steps. And in the Eucharist, the Lord makes us walk on his road, that of service, of sharing, of giving; and if it is shared, that little we have, that little we are, becomes riches, for the power of God—which is the power of love—comes down into our poverty to transform it.

So let us ask ourselves this evening, in adoring Christ who is really present in the Eucharist: do I let myself be transformed by him? Do I let the Lord who gives himself to me guide me to going out ever more from my little enclosure, in order to give, to share, to love him and others?

He Has Bent Down to Heal Us

Jesus understands human sufferings; he has shown the face of God's mercy, and he has bent down to heal body and soul. . . . This is his heart which looks to all of us, to our sicknesses, to our sins. The love of Jesus is great.

Seeing as Jesus Sees

Faith does not merely gaze at Jesus, but sees things as Jesus himself sees them, with his own eyes: it is a participation in his way of seeing. In many areas in our lives, we trust others who know more than we do. We trust the architect who builds our home, the pharmacist who gives us medicine for healing, the lawyer who defends us in court. We also need someone trustworthy and knowledgeable where God is concerned. Jesus, the Son of God, is the One who makes God known to us (cf. John 1:18). Christ's life, his way of knowing the Father and living in complete and constant relationship with him, opens up new and inviting vistas for human experience.

Believing in Jesus

St. John brings out the importance of a personal relationship with Jesus for our faith by using various forms of the verb "to believe." In addition to "believing that" what Jesus tells us is true, John also speaks of "believing" Jesus and "believing in" Jesus. We "believe" Jesus when we accept his word, his testimony, because he is truthful. We "believe in" Jesus when we personally welcome him into our lives and journey towards him, clinging to him in love and following in his footsteps along the way.

CHAPTER

3

GUIDED BY THE SPIRIT

Let the Spirit Speak to Your Heart

Let us allow ourselves to be guided by the Holy Spirit; let us allow him to speak to our hearts and say this to us: God is love, God is waiting for us, God is Father; he loves us as a true father loves; he loves us truly, and only the Holy Spirit can tell us this in our hearts. Let us hear the Holy Spirit, let us listen to the Holy Spirit, and may we move forward on this path of love, mercy, and forgiveness.

What Does the Spirit Tell You?

The Holy Spirit teaches us to see with the eyes of Christ, to live life as Christ lived, to understand life as Christ understood it. That is why the living water, who is the Holy Spirit, quenches our lives, why he tells us that we are loved by God as children, that we can love God as his children, and that by his grace, we can live as children of God, like Jesus. And we, do we listen to the Holy Spirit? What does the Holy Spirit tell us? He says: God loves you. He tells us this: God loves you, God likes you.

The Holy Spirit Teaches Us to Say "Papa"

In his Letter to the Romans, St. Paul wrote, "You have received the spirit of sonship. When we cry, 'Abba! Father!' it is the Spirit himself bearing witness with our spirit that we are children of God" (8:15-16).

It is the Spirit himself whom we received in Baptism, who teaches us, who spurs us to say to God, "Father" or rather, "Abba!" which means "Papa" or ["Dad"]. Our God is like this: he is a dad to us. The Holy Spirit creates within us this new condition as children of God. And this is the greatest gift we have received from the paschal mystery of Jesus.

The New Things of God

This is the work of the Holy Spirit: he brings us the new things of God. He comes to us and makes all things new; he changes us. The Spirit changes us! . . .

You see, the new things of God are not like the novelties of this world, all of which are temporary; they come and go, and we keep looking for more. The new things which God gives to our lives are lasting, not only in the future, when we will be with him, but today as well. God is even now making all things new; the Holy Spirit is truly transforming us, and through us he also wants to transform the world in which we live.

How Beautiful!

Let us open the doors to the Spirit; let ourselves be guided by him and allow God's constant help to make us new men and women, inspired by the love of God which the Holy Spirit bestows on us! How beautiful it would be if each of you, every evening, could say, "Today at school, at home, at work, guided by God, I showed a sign of love towards one of my friends, my parents, an older person!" How beautiful!

Are We Open to God's Surprises?

Newness always makes us a bit fearful, because we feel more secure if we have everything under control, if we are the ones who build, program, and plan our lives in accordance with our own ideas, our own comfort, our own preferences. This is also the case when it comes to God. Often we follow him, we accept him, but only up to a certain point. It is hard to abandon ourselves to him with complete trust, allowing the Holy Spirit to be the soul and guide of our lives in our every decision. We fear that God may force us to strike out on new paths and leave behind our all-too-narrow, closed, and selfish horizons in order to become open to his own. Yet throughout the history of salvation, whenever God reveals himself, he brings newness—God always brings newness— and demands our complete trust. . . .

The newness which God brings into our lives is something that actually brings fulfillment, that gives true joy, true serenity, because God loves us and desires only our good. Let us ask ourselves today:

are we open to "God's surprises"? Or are we closed and fearful before the newness of the Holy Spirit? Do we have the courage to strike out along the new paths which God's newness sets before us, or do we resist, barricaded in transient structures which have lost their capacity for openness to what is new? We would do well to ask ourselves these questions all through the day.

Thirsting for the Living Water

The Holy Spirit is the inexhaustible source of God's life in us. Man of every time and place desires a full and beautiful life, just and good, a life that is not threatened by death but can still mature and grow to fullness. Man is like a traveler who, crossing the deserts of life, thirsts for the living water: gushing and fresh, capable of quenching his deep desire for light, love, beauty, and peace. We all feel this desire! And Jesus gives us this living water: he is the Holy Spirit, who proceeds from the Father and whom Jesus pours out into our hearts. "I came that they may have life, and have it abundantly," Jesus tells us (John 10:10).

The Holy Spirit Creates Harmony

The Holy Spirit would appear to create disorder in the Church, since he brings the diversity of charisms and gifts. Yet all this, by his working, is a great source of wealth, for the Holy Spirit is the Spirit of unity, which does not mean uniformity, but which leads everything back to *harmony*. In the Church it is the Holy Spirit who creates harmony. One of the Fathers of the Church has an expression which I love: The Holy Spirit himself is harmony— *Ipse harmonia est*. He is indeed harmony. Only the Spirit can awaken diversity, plurality, and multiplicity while at the same time building unity.

Unity Is the Work of the Spirit

When we are the ones who try to create diversity and close ourselves up in what makes us different and other, we bring division. When we are the ones who want to build unity in accordance with our human plans, we end up creating uniformity, standardization. But if instead we let ourselves be guided by the Spirit, richness, variety, and diversity never become a source of conflict, because he impels us to experience variety within the communion of the Church.

The Gift of the Risen Christ

The life I now live in the flesh I live by faith in the Son of God, who loved me and gave himself for me" (Galatians 2:20). What is this life? It is God's own life. And who brings us this life? It is the Holy Spirit, the gift of the Risen Christ. The Spirit leads us into the divine life as true children of God, as sons and daughters in the only-begotten Son, Jesus Christ. Are we open to the Holy Spirit? Do we let ourselves be guided by him?

Chapter 4

TRUSTING IN GOD'S MERCY

The Courage to Go to Jesus

This is important: the courage to trust in Jesus' mercy, to trust in his patience, to seek refuge always in the wounds of his love. . . .

Maybe someone among us here is thinking: my sin is so great, I am as far from God as the younger son in the parable; my unbelief is like that of Thomas. I don't have the courage to go back, to believe that God can welcome me and that he is waiting for me, of all people. But God is indeed waiting for you; he asks of you only the courage to go to him.

How many times in my pastoral ministry have I heard it said, "Father, I have many sins," and I have always pleaded, "Don't be afraid; go to him; he is waiting for you; he will take care of everything." We hear many offers from the world around us, but let us take up God's offer instead: his is a caress of love.

Don't Be Afraid of Your Weakness

Three times [Peter] denied Jesus, precisely when he should have been closest to him; and when he hits bottom, he meets the gaze of Jesus, who patiently, wordlessly, says to him, "Peter, don't be afraid of your weakness; trust in me." Peter understands; he feels the loving gaze of Jesus, and he weeps. How beautiful is this gaze of Jesus—how much tenderness is there! Brothers and sisters, let us never lose trust in the patience and mercy of God!

He Never Tires of Forgiving Us

Let us not forget this word: God never, ever tires of forgiving us! . . . The problem is that we ourselves tire; we do not want to ask; we grow weary of asking for forgiveness. He never tires of forgiving, but at times we get tired of asking for forgiveness.

Let us never tire; let us never tire! He is the loving Father who always pardons, who has that heart of mercy for us all. And let us too learn to be merciful to everyone. Let us invoke the intercession of Our Lady who held in her arms the Mercy of God made man.

God Always Thinks with Mercy

God always thinks with mercy: do not forget this. God always thinks mercifully. He is the merciful Father! God thinks like the father waiting for the son and goes to meet him; he spots him coming when he is still far off [Luke 15:11-32]. . . .

What does this mean? That he went every day to see if his son was coming home: this is our merciful Father. It indicates that he was waiting for him with longing on the terrace of his house.

We Have an Advocate in Jesus

Jesus is our Advocate: how beautiful it is to hear this! When someone is summoned by the judge or is involved in legal proceedings, the first thing he does is to seek a lawyer to defend him. We have One who always defends us, who defends us from the snares of the devil, who defends us from ourselves and from our sins!

Dear brothers and sisters, we have this Advocate. Let us not be afraid to turn to him to ask forgiveness, to ask for a blessing, to ask for mercy! He always pardons us; he is our Advocate: he always defends us! Don't forget this!

Jesus' Mercy Gives Life

The mercy of Jesus is not only an emotion; it is a force which gives life that raises man! Today's Gospel also tells us this in the episode of the widow of Nain (Luke 7:11-17). With his disciples, Jesus arrives in Nain, a village in Galilee, right at the moment when a funeral is taking place. A boy, the only son of a widow, is being carried [out] for burial. Jesus immediately fixes his gaze on the crying mother. The Evangelist Luke says, "And when the Lord saw her, he had compassion on her" (7:13). This "compassion" is God's love for man; it is mercy, thus the attitude of God in contact with human misery, with our destitution, our suffering, our anguish. The biblical term "compassion" recalls a mother's womb. The mother, in fact, reacts in a way all her own in confronting the pain of her children. It is in this way, according to Scripture, that God loves us.

What is the fruit of this love and mercy? It is life! Jesus says to the widow of Nain, "Do not weep," and then he calls the dead boy and awakes him as if from sleep (cf. Luke 7:13-15). Let's think about this. It's beautiful: God's mercy gives life to man; it raises him from the dead. Let us not forget that the Lord always watches over us with mercy; he always watches over us with mercy. Let us not be afraid of approaching him! He has a merciful heart! If we show him our inner wounds, our inner sins, he will always forgive us. It is pure mercy. Let us go to Jesus!

God's Mercy Leads Us On

What a beautiful truth of faith this is for our lives: the mercy of God! God's love for us is so great, so deep; it is an unfailing love, one which always takes us by the hand and supports us, lifts us up, and leads us on.

The Lord's Most Powerful Message

Jesus has this message for us: mercy. I think—and I say it with humility—that this is the Lord's most powerful message: mercy. . . . But if we are like the Pharisee before the altar who said, "I thank you, Lord, that I am not like other men, and especially not like the one at the door, like that publican" (cf. Luke 18:11-12), then we do not know the Lord's heart, and we will never have the joy of experiencing this mercy!

"Lord, I Am Here"

Remember what St. Paul says: "What shall I boast of, if not my weakness, my poverty?" (cf. 2 Corinthians 11:30). Precisely in feeling my sinfulness, in looking at my sins, I can see and encounter God's mercy, his love, and go to him to receive forgiveness.

In my own life, I have so often seen God's merciful countenance, his patience. I have also seen so many people find the courage to enter the wounds of Jesus by saying to him, "Lord, I am here; accept my poverty, hide my sin in your wounds, wash it away with your blood." And I have always seen that God did just this—he accepted them, consoled them, cleansed them, loved them.

Dwelling in His Loving Wounds

Dear brothers and sisters, let us be enveloped by the mercy of God; let us trust in his patience, which always gives us more time. Let us find the courage to return to his house, to dwell in his loving wounds, allowing ourselves to be loved by him and to encounter his mercy in the sacraments. We will feel his wonderful tenderness, we will feel his embrace, and we, too, will become more capable of mercy, patience, forgiveness, and love.

The Lord Is There First!

We say we must seek God, go to him and ask forgiveness, but when we go, he is waiting for us; he is there first! In Spanish we have a word that explains this well: *primerear*—the Lord always gets there before us, he gets there first, he is waiting for us! To find someone waiting for you is truly a great grace. You go to him as a sinner, but he is waiting to forgive you. This is the experience that the prophets of Israel describe, comparing the Lord to the almond blossom, the first flower of spring (cf. Jeremiah 1:11-12). Before any other flowers appear, he is there, waiting. The Lord is waiting for us.

God, the Living One, Is Merciful!

Jesus allows a woman who is a sinner to approach him during a meal in the house of a Pharisee, scandalizing those present. Not only does he let the woman approach, but he even forgives her sins, saying, "Her sins, which are many, are forgiven, for she loved much; but he who is forgiven little, loves little" (Luke 7:47). Jesus is the incarnation of the Living God, the One who brings life amid so many deeds of death; amid sin, selfishness, and self-absorption. Jesus accepts, loves, uplifts, encourages, forgives, restores the ability to walk, gives back life. Throughout the Gospels we see how Jesus by his words and actions brings the transforming life of God. This was the experience of the woman who anointed the feet of the Lord with ointment: she felt understood, loved, and she responded by a gesture of love; she let herself be touched by God's mercy, she obtained forgiveness, and she started a new life. God, the Living One, is merciful. Do you agree? Let's say it together: God, the Living One, is merciful! All together now: God, the Living One, is merciful. Once again: God, the Living One, is merciful!

Peace Comes from God's Mercy

Peace be with you" (John 20:19, 21, 26). This is not a greeting, nor even a simple good wish; it is a gift, indeed, the precious gift that Christ offered his disciples after he had passed through death and hell.

He gives peace, as he had promised: "Peace I leave with you; my peace I give to you; not as the world gives do I give to you" (John 14:27). This peace is the fruit of the victory of God's love over evil; it is the fruit of forgiveness. And it really is like this: true peace, that profound peace, comes from experiencing God's mercy.

Great Is God's Mercy

Ah, brothers and sisters, God's face is the face of a merciful father who is always patient. Have you thought about God's patience, the patience he has with each one of us? That is his mercy. He always has patience, patience with us; he understands us, he waits for us, he does not tire of forgiving us if we are able to return to him with a contrite heart. "Great is God's mercy," says the psalm.

He Forgets, He Kisses You, He Embraces You

It is not easy to entrust oneself to God's mercy because it is an abyss beyond our comprehension. But we must! "Oh, Father, if you knew my life, you would not say that to me!" "Why, what have you done?" "Oh, I am a great sinner!" "All the better! Go to Jesus: he likes you to tell him these things!" He forgets; he has a very special capacity for forgetting. He forgets, he kisses you, he embraces you, and he simply says to you, "Neither do I condemn you; go, and sin no more" (cf. John 8:11). That is the only advice he gives you.

PROCLAIMING
THE GOSPEL

How Can We Not Share This Treasure?

We believe in the Risen One who conquered evil and death! Let us have the courage to "come out of ourselves," to take this joy and this light to all the places of our lives! The resurrection of Christ is our greatest certainty; he is our most precious treasure! How can we not share this treasure, this certainty with others? It is not only for us; it is to be passed on, to be shared with others. Our testimony is precisely this.

Passing on the Faith

I had the great blessing of growing up in a family in which faith was lived in a simple, practical way. However, it was my paternal grandmother, in particular, who influenced my journey of faith. She was a woman who explained to us, who talked to us about Jesus, who taught us the Catechism. I always remember that on the evening of Good Friday, she would take us to the candlelight procession, and at the end of this procession, "the dead Christ" would arrive, and our grandmother would make us—the children—kneel down, and she would say to us, "Look, he is dead, but tomorrow he will rise." This was how I received my first Christian proclamation, from this very woman, from my grandmother! This is really beautiful! The first proclamation at home, in the family!

And this makes me think of the love of so many mothers and grandmothers in the transmission of faith. They are the ones who pass on the faith. This used to happen in the early Church too, for St. Paul said to Timothy, "I am reminded of the faith of your mother and of your grandmother" (cf. 2 Timothy 1:5). All the mothers and all the grandmothers who are here should think about this: passing on the faith! Because God sets beside us people who help us on our journey of faith. We do not find our faith in the abstract, no! It is always a person preaching who tells us who Jesus is, who communicates faith to us and gives us the first proclamation. And this is how I received my first experience of faith.

Learning to Come Out of Ourselves

Following Jesus means learning to come out of ourselves . . . in order to go to meet others, to go toward the outskirts of existence, to be the first to take a step toward our brothers and our sisters, especially those who are the most distant, those who are forgotten, those who are most in need of understanding, comfort, and help. There is such a great need to bring the living presence of Jesus, merciful and full of love!

Preach with Your Life

Let us all remember this: one cannot proclaim the gospel of Jesus without the tangible witness of one's life. Those who listen to us and observe us must be able to see in our actions what they hear from our lips and so give glory to God! I am thinking now of some advice that St. Francis of Assisi gave to his brothers: preach the gospel and if necessary, use words. Preach with your life, with your witness.

God's Power to Evangelize

The mission that awaits us is, of course, challenging, but with the guidance of the Holy Spirit, it becomes an exciting one. We all experience our poverty, our weakness, in taking the precious treasure of the gospel to the world, but we must constantly repeat St. Paul's words: "We have this treasure in earthen vessels, to show that the transcendent power belongs to God and not to us" (2 Corinthians 4:7). It is this that must always give us courage: knowing that the power of evangelization comes from God, that it belongs to him. We are called to open ourselves more and more to the action of the Holy Spirit, to offer our unreserved readiness to be instruments of God's mercy, of his tenderness, of his love for every man and every woman and especially for the poor, the outcast, and those who are distant.

Furthermore, for every Christian, for the whole Church, this is not an optional mission; it is not an optional mission, but essential. As St. Paul said, "If I preach the gospel, that gives me no ground for boasting. For necessity is laid upon me. Woe to me if I do not preach the gospel!" (1 Corinthians 9:16). God's salvation is for everyone.

Be Missionaries of God's Mercy

Each individual Christian and every community is missionary to the extent that they bring to others and live the gospel and testify to God's love for all, especially those experiencing difficulties. Be missionaries of God's love and tenderness! Be missionaries of God's mercy, which always forgives us, always awaits us and loves us dearly.

Don't Stay in the Pen

Following and accompanying Christ, staying with him, demands "coming out of ourselves," requires us to be outgoing; to come out of ourselves, out of a dreary way of living faith that has become a habit, out of the temptation to withdraw into our own plans, which end by shutting out God's creative action.

God came out of himself to come among us; he pitched his tent among us to bring to us his mercy that saves and gives hope. Nor must we be satisfied with staying in the pen of the ninety-nine sheep if we want to follow him and to remain with him; we, too, must "go out" with him to seek the lost sheep, the one that has strayed the furthest. Be sure to remember: coming out of ourselves, just as Jesus, just as God came out of himself in Jesus, and Jesus came out of himself for all of us.

The Holy Spirit Is the Soul of Mission

The Holy Spirit is the soul of *mission*. The events that took place in Jerusalem almost two thousand years ago are not something far removed from us; they are events that affect us and become a lived experience in each of us. The Pentecost of the upper room in Jerusalem is the beginning, a beginning which endures. The Holy Spirit is the supreme gift of the Risen Christ to his apostles, yet he wants that gift to reach everyone. As we heard in the Gospel, Jesus says, "I will ask the Father, and he will give you another Advocate to remain with you forever" (cf. John 14:16). It is the Paraclete Spirit, the "Comforter," who grants us the courage to take to the streets of the world, bringing the gospel! The Holy Spirit makes us look to the horizon and drives us to the very outskirts of existence in order to proclaim life in Jesus Christ. Let us ask ourselves: do we tend to stay closed in on ourselves, on our group, or do we let the Holy Spirit open us to mission?

Witness Is What Counts!

Faith can only be communicated through witness, and that means love. Not with our own ideas but with the gospel, lived out in our own lives and brought to life within us by the Holy Spirit. There is, as it were, a synergy between us and the Holy Spirit, and this leads to witness. The Church is carried forward by the saints, who are the very ones who bear this witness. As both John Paul II and Benedict XVI have said, today's world stands in great need of witnesses, not so much of teachers, but rather of witnesses. It's not so much about speaking, but rather speaking with our whole lives: living consistently, the very consistency of our lives! This consistency means living Christianity as an encounter with Jesus that brings me to others, not just as a social label. In terms of society, this is how we are—we are Christians closed in on ourselves. No, not this! Witness is what counts!

My Humble Little Witness Matters

The testimony of faith comes in very many forms: just as in a great fresco, there is a variety of colors and shades, yet they are all important, even those which do not stand out. In God's great plan, every detail is important, even yours, even my humble little witness, even the hidden witness of those who live their faith with simplicity in everyday family relationships, work relationships, friendships.

The Holy Spirit Gives Us the Words to Say

Who is the real driving force of evangelization in our lives and in the Church? Paul VI wrote clearly: "It is the Holy Spirit who today, just as at the beginning of the Church, acts in every evangelizer who allows himself to be possessed and led by him. The Holy Spirit places on his lips the words which he could not find by himself, and at the same time, the Holy Spirit predisposes the soul of the hearer to be open and receptive to the Good News and to the kingdom being proclaimed" (*Evangeli Nuntiandi,* 75). To evangelize, therefore, it is necessary to open ourselves once again to the horizon of God's Spirit, without being afraid of what he asks us or of where he leads us. Let us entrust ourselves to him! He will enable us to live out and bear witness to our faith, and will illuminate the heart of those we meet.

The Holy Spirit Drives Us Forward

The older theologians used to say that the soul is a kind of sailboat; the Holy Spirit is the wind that fills its sails and drives it forward, and the gusts of wind are the gifts of the Spirit. Lacking his impulse and his grace, we do not go forward. The Holy Spirit draws us into the mystery of the living God and saves us from the threat of a Church which is gnostic and self-referential, closed in on herself; he impels us to open the doors and go forth to proclaim and bear witness to the good news of the gospel, to communicate the joy of faith, the encounter with Christ.

Evangelizing Gives Us Joy

[On the day of Pentecost] Peter, filled with the Holy Spirit and "standing with the eleven, lifted up his voice" and "confidently" (Acts 2:14, 29) proclaimed the good news of Jesus, who gave his life for our salvation and whom God raised from the dead. This is another effect of the Holy Spirit's action: the courage to proclaim the newness of the gospel of Jesus to all, confidently (with *parrhesia*), in a loud voice, in every time and in every place.

Today too, this happens for the Church and for each one of us: the fire of Pentecost, from the action of the Holy Spirit, releases an ever new energy for mission, new ways in which to proclaim the message of salvation, new courage for evangelizing. Let us never close ourselves to this action! Let us live the gospel humbly and courageously!

Let us witness to the newness, hope, and joy that the Lord brings to life. Let us feel within us "the delightful and comforting joy of evangelizing"

(*Evangelii Nuntiandi,* 80). Because evangelizing, proclaiming Jesus, gives us joy. Instead, egoism makes us bitter, sad, and depresses us. Evangelizing uplifts us.

We Are the Simple Instruments of God

It is urgently necessary to find new forms and new ways to ensure that God's grace may touch the heart of every man and of every woman and lead them to him. We are all simple but important instruments of his; we have not received the gift of faith to keep it hidden but rather to spread it so that it can illumine a great many of our brethren on their journey.

Martyrdom: The Highest Degree of Witness

To proclaim the gospel, two virtues are essential: courage and patience [acceptance of suffering]. They [Christians who are suffering] are in the Church of "patience." They suffer, and there are more martyrs today than there were in the early centuries of the Church. More martyrs! Our own brothers and sisters. They are suffering! They carry their faith even to martyrdom. However, martyrdom is never a defeat; martyrdom is the highest degree of the witness we must give. We are on the way to martyrdom, as small martyrs: giving up this, doing that . . . but we are on the way. And they, poor things, they give their lives, but they do so . . . for love of Jesus, witnessing to Jesus.

The Motivation of Mission

When I was studying theology, I wrote to the [Superior] General [of the Jesuits], who was Fr. Arrupe, asking him to dispatch me, to send me to Japan or to some other place. However, he thought about it at length and said to me, with great kindness, "But you have had a lung disease, which is not very good for such demanding work," so I stayed in Buenos Aires. Fr. Arrupe was so kind because he did not say, "But you are not holy enough to become a missionary"—he was kind; he was charitable. It was the dimension of mission that gave me such great determination to be a Jesuit: to go out, to go to the missions and proclaim Jesus Christ. I believe this is a feature specific to our spirituality: to go out, to go out to always proclaim Jesus Christ, and to never stay somehow closed in our structures, which are so often transient. This is what motivated me.

CHAPTER

6

DON'T FORGET
THE POOR

The Scandal of Poverty

The times speak to us of such great poverty throughout the world, and this is a scandal. The poverty of the world is a scandal. In a world where there is such great wealth, so many resources for giving food to everyone, it is impossible to understand how there could be so many hungry children, so many children without education, so many poor people! Poverty today is a cry. We must all think about whether we can become a little poorer. This is something we must all do. How can I become a little poorer, to be more like Jesus, who was the poor Teacher?

A Church Poor and for the Poor

Some people wanted to know why the Bishop of Rome wished to be called Francis. Some thought of Francis Xavier, Francis de Sales, and also Francis of Assisi. I will tell you the story. During the election, I was seated next to the Archbishop Emeritus of São Paolo and Prefect Emeritus of the Congregation for the Clergy, Cardinal Claudio Hummes, a good friend, a good friend! When things were looking dangerous, he encouraged me. And when the votes reached two-thirds, there was the usual applause, because the pope had been elected. And he gave me a hug and a kiss, and said, "Don't forget the poor!" And those words came to me: the poor, the poor. Then, right away, thinking of the poor, I thought of Francis of Assisi. Then I thought of all the wars, as the votes were still being counted, till the end. Francis is also the man of peace. That is how the name came into my heart: Francis of Assisi. For me, he is the man of poverty, the man of peace, the man who loves and protects creation; these days we do not have a very good relationship with creation, do we? He is the man who gives us this spirit of peace, the poor man. . . . How I would like a Church which is poor and for the poor!

Money Has to Serve, Not Rule

Money has to serve, not rule! The pope loves everyone, rich and poor alike, but the pope has the duty, in Christ's name, to remind the rich to help the poor, to respect them, to promote them. The pope appeals for disinterested solidarity and for a return to person-centered ethics in the world of finance and economics.

Touching the Flesh of Christ

When I used to go to hear confessions in my previous diocese, people would come to me, and I would always ask them, "Do you give alms?" "Yes, Father!" "Very good." And I would ask them two further questions: "Tell me, when you give alms, do you look the person in the eye?" "Oh, I don't know; I haven't really thought about it." The second question: "And when you give alms, do you touch the hand of the person you are giving them to, or do you toss the coin at him or her?" This is the problem: the flesh of Christ, touching the flesh of Christ, taking upon ourselves this suffering for the poor. Poverty for us Christians is not a sociological, philosophical, or cultural category, no. It is theological. I might say this is the first category, because our God, the Son of God, abased himself; he made himself poor to walk along the road with us.

This is our poverty: the poverty of the flesh of Christ, the poverty that brought the Son of God to us through his incarnation. A poor Church for the poor begins by reaching out to the flesh of Christ. If we reach out to the flesh of Christ, we begin to understand something, to understand what this poverty, the Lord's poverty, actually is; and this is far from easy.

Poverty Demands That We Have Hope

Who robs you of hope? The spirit of the world, wealth, the spirit of vanity, arrogance, pride. All these things steal hope from you. Where do I find hope? In the poor Jesus, Jesus who made himself poor for us. . . . Poverty demands that we sow hope. It requires me to have greater hope, too. . . .

It is impossible to talk about poverty, about abstract poverty. That does not exist! Poverty is the flesh of the poor Jesus in this hungry child, in the sick person, in these unjust social structures. Go, look over there at the flesh of Jesus. But do not let yourselves be robbed of hope by well-being, by the spirit of well-being, which in the end brings you to become a nothing in life! The young must stake themselves on high ideals: this is my advice. But where do I find hope? In the flesh of the suffering Jesus and in true poverty. There is a connection between the two.

The Real Crisis

Right now, the whole world is in crisis. And crisis is not a bad thing. It is true that the crisis causes us suffering but we—and first and foremost, all you young people—must know how to interpret the crisis. What does this crisis mean? What must I do to help us to come through this crisis? The crisis we are experiencing at this time is a human crisis. People say: it is an economic crisis; it is a crisis of work. Yes, that's true. But why? This work problem, this problem in the economy, is a consequence of the great human problem. What is in crisis is the value of the human person, and we must defend the human person. . . .

Today the person counts for nothing; it is coins, it is money that counts. And Jesus, God, gave the world, the whole creation, to the person, to men and women that they might care for it; he did not give it to money. It is a crisis; the person is in a crisis because today—listen carefully, it is true—the person is a slave! We must liberate ourselves from these economic and social structures that enslave us. This is your duty.

The Sin of Indifference

Today no one in our world feels responsible; we have lost a sense of responsibility for our brothers and sisters. We have fallen into the hypocrisy of the priest and the Levite whom Jesus described in the parable of the Good Samaritan: we see our brother half-dead on the side of the road, and perhaps we say to ourselves, "Poor soul . . . !" and then go on our way. It's not our responsibility, and with that we feel reassured, assuaged. The culture of comfort, which makes us think only of ourselves, makes us insensitive to the cries of other people, makes us live in soap bubbles which, however lovely, are insubstantial; they offer a fleeting and empty illusion which results in indifference to others; indeed, it even leads to the globalization of indifference. In this globalized world, we have fallen into globalized indifference. We have become used to the suffering of others: it doesn't affect me; it doesn't concern me; it's none of my business!

Has Anyone Wept in Our World Today?

We are a society which has forgotten how to weep, how to experience compassion— "suffering with" others: the globalization of indifference has taken from us the ability to weep! In the Gospel we have heard the crying, the wailing, the great lamentation: "Rachel weeps for her children . . . because they are no more" (Matthew 2:18). Herod sowed death to protect his own comfort, his own soap bubble. And so it continues. . . . Let us ask the Lord to remove the part of Herod that lurks in our hearts; let us ask the Lord for the grace to weep over our indifference, to weep over the cruelty of our world, of our own hearts, and of all those who in anonymity make social and economic decisions which open the door to tragic situations like this. "Has anyone wept?" Today, has anyone wept in our world?

MOTHER MARY,
HELP US

Mary Shows Us How to Live in the Spirit

The Virgin Mary teaches us what it means to live in the Holy Spirit and what it means to accept the news of God in our lives. She conceived Jesus by the work of the Holy Spirit, and every Christian, each one of us, is called to accept the Word of God, to accept Jesus inside of us, and then to bring him to everyone. Mary invoked the Holy Spirit with the apostles in the upper room; we, too, every time that we come together in prayer, are sustained by the spiritual presence of the Mother of Jesus in order to receive the gift of the Spirit and to have the strength to witness to Jesus risen. . . . May Mary help you to be attentive to what the Lord asks of you and to live and walk forever with the Holy Spirit!

She Always Hurries to Us

Our Lady, as soon as she had heard the news that she was to be the Mother of Jesus and the announcement that her cousin Elizabeth was expecting a child—the Gospel says—she went to her in haste; she did not wait. She did not say, "But now I am with child; I must take care of my health; my cousin is bound to have friends who can care for her." Something stirred her and she "went with haste" to Elizabeth (Luke 1:39). It is beautiful to think this of Our Lady, of our Mother, that she hastens, because she intends to help. She goes to help; she doesn't go to boast and tell her cousin, "Listen, I'm in charge now, because I am the Mother of God!" No, she did not do that. She went to help! And Our Lady is always like this. She is our Mother who always hurries to us whenever we are in need.

It would be beautiful to add to the Litany of Our Lady something like this: "O Lady who goes in haste, pray for us!" It is lovely, isn't it? For she always goes in haste; she does not forget her children. And when her children are in difficulty, when they need something and call on her, she hurries to them. This gives us a security, the security of always having our Mother next to us, beside us. We move forward, we journey more easily in life, when our mother is near. Let us think of this grace of Our Lady, this grace that she gives us: of being close to us, but without making us wait for her. Always! She—let us trust in this—she lives to help us: Our Lady who always hastens, for our sake.

Mary's Example: Love God and Neighbor

The Holy Virgin made of her existence an unceasing and beautiful gift to God because she loved the Lord. Mary's example is an incentive . . . for all of us to live in charity for our neighbor, not out of some sort of social duty, but beginning from the love of God, from the charity of God. And also, . . . Mary is the one who leads us to Jesus and teaches us how to go to Jesus; and the Mother of Jesus is our own and makes a family, with us and with Jesus.

Our Lady Helps Us Grow Strong

A mother helps her children grow up and wants them to grow strong; that is why she teaches them not to be lazy—which can also derive from a certain kind of well-being—[and] not to sink into a comfortable lifestyle, contenting oneself with possessions. The mother takes care that her children develop better, that they grow strong, capable of accepting responsibilities, of engaging in life, of striving for great ideals. The Gospel of St Luke tells us that in the family of Nazareth, Jesus "grew and became strong, filled with wisdom; and the favor of God was upon him" (2:40). Our Lady does just this for us; she helps us to grow as human beings and in the faith, to be strong and never to fall into the temptation of being human beings and Christians in a superficial way, but to live responsibly, to strive ever higher.

Mary Teaches Us to Make Good Decisions

A good mother not only accompanies her children in their growth, without avoiding the problems and challenges of life; a good mother also helps them *to make definitive decisions with freedom*. This is not easy, but a mother knows how to do it. But what does freedom mean? It is certainly not doing whatever you want, allowing yourself to be dominated by the passions, to pass from one experience to another without discernment, to follow the fashions of the day; freedom does not mean, so to speak, throwing everything that you don't like out the window. No, that is not freedom! Freedom is given to us so that we know how to make good decisions in life! Mary as a good mother teaches us to be, like her, capable of making definitive decisions; definitive choices, at this moment in a time controlled by, so to speak, a philosophy of the provisional. It is very difficult to make a lifetime commitment. And she helps us to make those definitive decisions in the full freedom with which she said "yes" to the plan God had for her life (cf. Luke 1:38).

The Lord Entrusts Us to His Mother

Jesus from the cross says to Mary, indicating John, "Woman, behold your son!" and to John, "Here is your mother!" (cf. John 19:26, 27). In that disciple we are all represented: the Lord entrusts us to the loving and tender hands of the Mother, that we might feel her support in facing and overcoming the difficulties of our human and Christian journey; to never be afraid of the struggle, to face it with the help of the Mother.

A Prayer to Mary

Mary, *woman of listening*, open our ears; grant us to know how to listen to the word of your Son Jesus among the thousands of words of this world; grant that we may listen to the reality in which we live, to every person we encounter, especially those who are poor, in need, in hardship.

Mary, woman of decision, illuminate our mind and our heart so that we may obey, unhesitating, the word of your Son Jesus; give us the courage to decide, not to let ourselves be dragged along, letting others direct our life.

Mary, woman of action, [may] our hands and feet move "with haste" toward others, to bring them the charity and love of your Son Jesus, to bring the light of the gospel to the world, as you did. Amen.

CHAPTER
8

GIFTS OF FAITH, HOPE, AND JOY

Faith Lights Our Way

There is an urgent need . . . to see once again that faith is a light, for once the flame of faith dies out, all other lights begin to dim. The light of faith is unique, since it is capable of illuminating *every aspect* of human existence. For a light to be this powerful, it cannot come from ourselves; it must come from a more primordial source: in a word, it must come from God. Faith is born of an encounter with the living God who calls us and reveals his love, a love which precedes us and upon which we can lean for security and for building our lives. Transformed by this love, we gain fresh vision, new eyes to see; we realize that it contains a great promise of fulfillment, and that a vision of the future opens up before us. Faith, received from God as a supernatural gift, becomes a light for our way, guiding our journey through time.

The Beatitude of Faith

Thomas exclaimed, "My Lord and my God!" (John 20:28). So Jesus said, "Have you believed because you have seen me? Blessed are those who have not seen and yet believe" (20:29); and who were those who believed without seeing? Other disciples, other men and women of Jerusalem who, on the testimony of the apostles and the women, believed even though they had not met the Risen Jesus. This is a very important word about faith; we can call it the *beatitude of faith*. Blessed are those who have not seen but have believed: this is the beatitude of faith! In every epoch and in every place, blessed are those who, on the strength of the word of God proclaimed in the Church and witnessed by Christians, believe that Jesus Christ is the love of God incarnate, Mercy incarnate. And this applies for each one of us!

Faith Is Linked to Hope

Suffering reminds us that faith's service to the common good is always one of hope—a hope which looks ever ahead in the knowledge that only from God, from the future which comes from the Risen Jesus, can our society find solid and lasting foundations. In this sense, faith is linked to hope, for even if our dwelling place here below is wasting away, we have an eternal dwelling place which God has already prepared in Christ, in his body (cf. 2 Corinthians 4:16-5:5).

A Gift That Demands Response

Faith is first of all a gift we have received. But in order to bear fruit, God's grace always demands our openness to him, our free and tangible response. Christ comes to bring us the mercy of a God who saves. We are asked to trust in him, to correspond to the gift of his love with a good life, made up of actions motivated by faith and love.

The Joy of Being Carried by Jesus

Let us follow Jesus! We accompany, we follow Jesus, but above all we know that he accompanies us and carries us on his shoulders. This is our joy; this is the hope that we must bring to this world. Please do not let yourselves be robbed of hope! Do not let hope be stolen—the hope that Jesus gives us!

Our Hope Is Safe and Sound

The Risen Lord is the hope that never fails, that never disappoints (cf. Romans 5:5). Hope does not let us down—the hope of the Lord! How often in our life do hopes vanish; how often do the expectations we have in our hearts come to nothing! Our hope as Christians is strong, safe, and sound on this earth where God has called us to walk, and it is open to eternity because it is founded on God who is always faithful. We must not forget: God is always faithful to us. Being raised with Christ through Baptism, with the gift of faith, an inheritance that is incorruptible, prompts us to seek God's things more often, to think of him more often and to pray to him more.

The Joy of Being Children of God

Let us point out the Risen Christ to those who ask us to account for the hope that is in us (cf. 1 Peter 3:15). Let us point him out with the proclamation of the word, but above all with our lives as people who have been raised. Let us show the joy of being children of God, the freedom that living in Christ gives us, which is true freedom, the freedom that saves us from the slavery of evil, of sin, and of death! Looking at the heavenly homeland, we shall receive new light and fresh strength, both in our commitment and in our daily efforts.

Remember What God Has Done for You

To remember what God has done and continues to do for me, for us, to remember the road we have traveled: this is what opens our hearts to hope for the future. May we learn to remember everything that God has done in our lives.

The Courage to Swim Against the Tide

Remain steadfast in the journey of faith, with firm hope in the Lord. This is the secret of our journey! He gives us the courage to swim against the tide . . . to go against the current; this is good for the heart, but we need courage to swim against the tide. Jesus gives us this courage!

A Christian Can Never Be Sad

Do not be men and women of sadness; a Christian can never be sad! Never give way to discouragement! Ours is a joy born not of having many possessions but from having encountered a Person: Jesus, in our midst. It is born from knowing that with him we are never alone, even at difficult moments, even when our life's journey comes up against problems and obstacles that seem insurmountable, and there are so many of them!

The Resurrection Opens Us to Hope

The death and resurrection of Jesus are the heart of our hope. The apostle [Paul] said, "If Christ has not been raised, your faith is futile and you are still in your sins" (1 Corinthians 15:17). Unfortunately, efforts have often been made to blur faith in the resurrection of Jesus and doubts have crept in, even among believers. It is a little like that "rosewater" faith, as we say; it is not a strong faith. And this is due to superficiality and sometimes to indifference, busy as we are with a thousand things considered more important than faith, or because we have a view of life that is solely horizontal. However, it is the resurrection itself that opens us to greater hope, for it opens our lives and the life of the world to the eternal future of God, to full happiness, to the certainty that evil, sin, and death may be overcome.

CHAPTER

9

PRAY EVERY DAY

Give God Space in Prayer

In the silence of the daily routine, St. Joseph, together with Mary, shares a single common center of attention: Jesus. They accompany and nurture the growth of the Son of God made man for us with commitment and tenderness, reflecting on everything that has happened. In the Gospels, St. Luke twice emphasizes the attitude of Mary, which is also that of St. Joseph: she "kept all these things, pondering them in her heart" (2:19, 51). To listen to the Lord, we must learn to contemplate, feel his constant presence in our lives, and we must stop and converse with him, give him space in prayer. Each of us . . . should ask ourselves, "How much space do I give to the Lord? Do I stop to talk with him?" Ever since we were children, our parents have taught us to start and end the day with a prayer, to teach us to feel that the friendship and the love of God accompany us. Let us remember the Lord more in our daily life!

Let the Lord Look at You

The Lord looks at us. He looks at us first. My experience is what I feel in front of the tabernacle, when I go in the evening to pray before the Lord. Sometimes I nod off for a while; this is true, for the strain of the day more or less makes you fall asleep, but he understands. I feel great comfort when I think of the Lord looking at me. We think we have to pray and talk, talk, talk. . . . No! Let the Lord look at you. When he looks at us, he gives us strength and helps us to bear witness to him.

Give God First Place

Worshipping the Lord means giving him the place that he must have; worshipping the Lord means stating, believing—not only by our words—that he alone truly guides our lives; worshipping the Lord means that we are convinced before him that he is the only God, the God of our lives, the God of our history.

Pray to the Spirit

This is a prayer we must pray every day: "Holy Spirit, make my heart open to the word of God; make my heart open to goodness; make my heart open to the beauty of God every day." I would like to ask everyone a question: how many of you pray every day to the Holy Spirit? There will not be many, but we must fulfill Jesus' wish and pray every day to the Holy Spirit, that he open our hearts to Jesus.

Take a Step Toward the Law of Love

Oh, how much more of the journey do we have to make in order to actually live the new law— the law of the Holy Spirit who acts in us, the law of charity, of love! Looking in newspapers or on television, we see so many wars between Christians: how does this happen? Within the People of God, there are so many wars! How many wars of envy, of jealousy, are waged in neighborhoods, in the workplace! Even within the family itself, there are so many internal wars! We must ask the Lord to make us correctly understand this law of love. How beautiful it is to love one another as true brothers and sisters. How beautiful! Let's do something today. We may all have likes and dislikes; many of us are perhaps a little angry with someone. Then let us say to the Lord, "Lord, I am angry with this or that person; I am praying to you for him or her." To pray for those with whom we are angry is a beautiful step toward that law of love. Shall we take it? Let's take it today!

Mission and Prayer

"Pray therefore the Lord of the harvest to send out laborers into his harvest" (Luke 10:2). The laborers for the harvest are not chosen through advertising campaigns or appeals of service and generosity, but they are "chosen" and "sent" by God. It is he who chooses, it is he who sends, it is the Lord who sends, it is he who gives the mission. For this, prayer is important. The Church, as Benedict XVI has often reiterated, is not ours, but God's; and how many times do we, consecrated men and women, think that the Church is ours! We make of it . . . something that we invent in our minds. But it is not ours!—it is God's. The field to be cultivated is his. The mission is grace. And if the apostle is born of prayer, he finds in prayer the light and strength of his action. Our mission ceases to bear fruit; indeed, it is extinguished the moment the link with its source, with the Lord, is interrupted.

THE CHURCH IS
OUR FAMILY

The Church Is Born from the Cross

So what is the Church born from? She is born from the supreme act of love of the cross, from the pierced side of Jesus from which flowed blood and water, a symbol of the sacraments of the Eucharist and of Baptism. The lifeblood of God's family, of the Church, is God's love, which is actualized in loving him and others, all others, without distinction or reservation. The Church is a family in which we love and are loved.

Pray for the Church

Let us ask ourselves today: how much do I love the Church? Do I pray for her? Do I feel part of the family of the Church? What do I do to ensure that she is a community in which each one feels welcomed and understood, feels the mercy and love of God who renews life? Faith is a gift and an act which concern us personally, but God calls us to live with our faith together, as a family, as Church.

Let us ask the Lord . . . that our communities, the whole Church, be increasingly true families that live and bring the warmth of God.

The Lord Invites Us into the People of God

What does "People of God" mean? First of all, it means that God does not belong in a special way to any one people, for it is he who calls us, convokes us, invites us to be part of his people, and this invitation is addressed to all, without distinction, for the mercy of God "desires all men to be saved" (1 Timothy 2:4). Jesus does not tell the apostles or us to form an exclusive group, a group of the *elite*. Jesus says, "Go out and make disciples of all people" (cf. Matthew 28:19). St. Paul says that in the People of God, in the Church, "there is neither Jew nor Greek . . . for you are all one in Christ Jesus" (Galatians 3:28). I would also like to say to anyone who feels far away from God and the Church, to anyone who is timid or indifferent, to those who think they can no longer change: the Lord calls you too to become part of his people, and he does this with great respect and love! He invites us to be part of this people, the People of God!

The Leaven of God

Dear brothers and sisters, being the Church, to be the People of God in accordance with the Father's great design of love, means to be the leaven of God in this humanity of ours. It means to proclaim and to bring God's salvation to this world of ours so often led astray and in need of answers that give courage, hope, and new vigor for the journey. May the Church be a place of God's mercy and hope, where all feel welcomed, loved, forgiven, and encouraged to live according to the good life of the gospel. And to make others feel welcomed, loved, forgiven, and encouraged, the Church must be with doors wide open so that all may enter. And we must go out through these doors and proclaim the gospel.

The Church Is Not a Political Movement

The Church is neither a political movement nor a well-organized structure. That is not what she is. We are not an NGO [nongovernmental organization], and when the Church becomes an NGO, she loses her salt, she has no savor, she is only an empty organization.

We need cunning here, because the devil deceives us and we risk falling into the trap of hyperefficiency. Preaching Jesus is one thing; attaining goals, being efficient, is another. No, efficiency is a different value. Basically, the value of the Church is living by the gospel and witnessing to our faith. The Church is the salt of the earth; she is the light of the world. She is called to make present in society the leaven of the kingdom of God, and she does this primarily with her witness, the witness of brotherly love, of solidarity, and of sharing with others.

The Church Is a Living Body

The Church is not a welfare, cultural, or political association but a living body that walks and acts in history. And this body has a head, Jesus, who guides, feeds, and supports it. This is a point that I would like to emphasize: if one separates the head from the rest of the body, the whole person cannot survive. It is like this in the Church: we must stay ever more deeply connected with Jesus. But not only that; just as it is important that lifeblood flow through the body in order to live, so must we allow Jesus to work in us, let his word guide us, his presence in the Eucharist feed us and give us life, his love strengthen our love for our neighbor. And this forever! Forever and ever!

Why Are Christians Divided?

So much damage to the Church comes from division among Christians, from biases, from narrow interests. Division among us, but also division among communities: Evangelical Christians, Orthodox Christians, Catholic Christians. Why are we divided? We must try to bring about unity. I will tell you something: today, before leaving home, I spent forty minutes, more or less, . . . with an Evangelical pastor, and we prayed together and sought unity. Because we have to pray, together as Catholics and also with other Christians, pray that the Lord give us the gift of unity, unity among us. But how will we have unity among Christians if we are not capable of it among ourselves, as Catholics? Or in our families? So many families fight and are divided! Seek unity, the unity that builds the Church. Unity comes from Jesus Christ. He sends us the Holy Spirit to create unity.

An Ecumenism of Suffering

If one member suffers, all suffer together; if one member is honored, all rejoice together" (1 Corinthians 12:26). This is a law of the Christian life, and in this sense, we can say that there is also an ecumenism of suffering: just as the blood of the martyrs was a seed of strength and fertility for the Church, so too the sharing of daily sufferings can become an effective instrument of unity. And this also applies, in a certain sense, to the broader context of society and relations between Christians and non-Christians: from shared suffering can blossom forth forgiveness, reconciliation, and peace, with God's help.

The Church Exists to Evangelize

In the Creed, immediately after professing our faith in the Holy Spirit, we say, "I believe in one, holy, catholic and apostolic Church." There is a profound connection between these two realities of faith: indeed, it is the Holy Spirit who gives life to the Church, who guides her steps. Without the constant presence and action of the Holy Spirit, the Church could not live and could not carry out the task that the Risen Jesus entrusted to her: to go and make disciples of all nations (cf. Matthew 28:19).

Evangelizing is the Church's mission. It is not the mission of only a few, but it is mine, yours, and our mission. The apostle Paul exclaimed, "Woe to me if I do not preach the gospel!" (1 Corinthians 9:16). We must all be evangelizers, especially with our life! Paul VI stressed that "evangelizing is . . . the grace and vocation proper to the Church, her deepest identity. She exists in order to evangelize" (*Evangeli Nuntiandi,* 14).

The Church's Witness of Brotherly Love

When a person truly knows Jesus Christ and believes in him, that person experiences his presence in life as well as the power of his resurrection, and cannot but communicate this experience. And if this person meets with misunderstanding or adversity, he behaves like Jesus in his passion: he answers with love and with the power of the truth.

. . . Let us ask for the help of Mary Most Holy so that the Church throughout the world may proclaim the resurrection of the Lord with candor and courage and give credible witness to it with signs of brotherly love. Brotherly love is the closest testimony we can give that Jesus is alive with us, that Jesus is risen.

Body and Limb Must Be United!

St. Paul says that just as the limbs of the human body, although diverse and many, form one body, so have we been baptized by one Spirit into one body (cf. 1 Corinthians 12:12-13). Consequently, in the Church there is variety and a diversity of roles and functions; there is no flat uniformity but a wealth of gifts that the Holy Spirit distributes. Yet there is communion and unity: each one relates to the other and comes together to form a single living body, deeply tied to Christ. Let us remember this well: being part of the Church means being united to Christ and receiving from him the divine life that makes us live as Christians; it means staying united to the pope and to the bishops who are instruments of unity and communion; and it also means learning to overcome subjectivism and division, to understand each other better, to harmonize the variety and the richness of each person—in a word, to love God and the people beside us more, in the family, in the parish, in associations. Body and limb, in order to live, must be united! Unity is superior to conflict, always!

Do Not Fear Solidarity

Where does the multiplication of the loaves come from? The answer lies in Jesus' request to the disciples: "You give them . . . ," "to give," to share. What do the disciples share? The little they have: five loaves and two fish. However, it is those very loaves and fish in the Lord's hands that feed the entire crowd. And it is the disciples themselves, bewildered as they face the insufficiency of their means, the poverty of what they are able to make available, who get the people to sit down and who—trusting in Jesus' words—distribute the loaves and fish that satisfy the crowd. And this tells us that in the Church, but also in society, a key word of which we must not be frightened is "solidarity," that is, the ability to make what we have, our humble capacities, available to God. For only in sharing, in giving, will our lives be fruitful. Solidarity is a word seen badly by the spirit of the world!

Are We Living Stones?

How do we live our being Church? Are we living stones, or are we, as it were, stones that are weary, bored, or indifferent? Have you ever noticed how grim it is to see a tired, bored, and indifferent Christian? A Christian like that is all wrong; the Christian must be alive, rejoicing in being Christian; he or she must live this beauty of belonging to the People of God which is the Church. Do we open ourselves to the action of the Holy Spirit, to be an active part of our communities, or do we withdraw into ourselves, saying, "I have so much to do; it isn't my job!"?

The Lord gives all of us his grace, his strength, so that we may be profoundly united to Christ, who is the cornerstone, the pillar and the foundation of our life and of the whole life of the Church. Let us pray that enlivened by his Spirit, we may always be living stones of his Church.

We Are All Equal in the Church

What does the Holy Spirit do among us? He designs the variety which is a wealth in the Church and unites us, each and every one, to constitute a spiritual temple in which we do not offer material sacrifices but ourselves, our life (cf. 1 Peter 2:4-5). The Church is not a fabric woven of things and interests; she is the Temple of the Holy Spirit, the Temple in which God works, the Temple in which, with the gift of Baptism, each one of us is a living stone. This tells us that no one in the Church is useless, and if from time to time someone says to someone else, "Go home, you are no good," this is not true. For no one is no good in the Church; we are all necessary for building this Temple! No one is secondary. No one is the most important person in the Church; we are all equal in God's eyes. Some of you might say, "Listen, Mr. Pope, you are not our equal." Yes, I am like each one of you; we are all equal, we are brothers and sisters!

We Can't Believe on Our Own

It is impossible to believe on our own. Faith is not simply an individual decision which takes place in the depths of the believer's heart, nor a completely private relationship between the "I" of the believer and the divine "Thou," between an autonomous subject and God. By its very nature, faith is open to the "We" of the Church; it always takes place within her communion.

CHAPTER

11

DEALING WITH TRIALS AND TEMPTATIONS

God Grants Strength to Our Weakness

There are no difficulties, trials, or misunderstandings to fear, provided we remain united to God as branches to the vine, provided we do not lose our friendship with him, provided we make ever more room for him in our lives. This is especially so whenever we feel poor, weak, and sinful, because God grants strength to our weakness, riches to our poverty, conversion and forgiveness to our sinfulness.

God Can Change Any Situation

Let us not be closed to the newness that God wants to bring into our lives! Are we often weary, disheartened, and sad? Do we feel weighed down by our sins? Do we think that we won't be able to cope? Let us not close our hearts; let us not lose confidence; let us never give up. There are no situations which God cannot change; there is no sin which he cannot forgive if only we open ourselves to him.

Stripping Ourselves of Idols

We have to empty ourselves of the many small or great idols which we have and in which we take refuge, on which we often seek to base our security. They are idols which we sometimes keep well-hidden; they can be ambition, careerism, a taste for success, placing ourselves at the center, the tendency to dominate others, the claim to be the sole masters of our lives, some sins to which we are bound, and many others. This evening I would like a question to resound in the hearts of each one of you, and I would like you to answer it honestly: have I considered which idol lies hidden in my life that prevents me from worshipping the Lord? Worshipping is stripping ourselves of our idols, even the most hidden ones, and choosing the Lord as the center, as the highway of our lives.

Trials Lead to God's Glory

We must undergo many trials if we are to enter the kingdom of God (cf. Acts 14:22). The journey of the Church and our own personal journeys as Christians are not always easy; they meet with difficulties and trials. To follow the Lord, to let his Spirit transform the shadowy parts of our lives, our ungodly ways of acting, and cleanse us of our sins, is to set out on a path with many obstacles, both in the world around us but also within us, in the heart. But difficulties and trials are part of the path that leads to God's glory, just as they were for Jesus who was glorified on the cross; we will always encounter them in life! Do not be discouraged! We have the power of the Holy Spirit to overcome these trials!

Do Not Fear Commitment

Temporary things seduce us. We are victims of a trend that pushes us to the provisional . . . as though we wanted to stay adolescents. There is a little charm in staying adolescents, and this for life! Let us not be afraid of life commitments, commitments that take up and concern our entire life! In this way our life will be fruitful! And this is freedom: to have the courage to make these decisions with generosity.

Choose Life

All too often, as we know from experience, people do not choose life; they do not accept the "Gospel of Life" but let themselves be led by ideologies and ways of thinking that block life, that do not respect life, because they are dictated by selfishness, self-interest, profit, power, and pleasure and not by love, by concern for the good of others. It is the eternal dream of wanting to build the city of man without God, without God's life and love—a new Tower of Babel. It is the idea that rejecting God, the message of Christ, the Gospel of Life, will somehow lead to freedom, to complete human fulfillment. As a result, the Living God is replaced by fleeting human idols which offer the intoxication of a flash of freedom but in the end bring new forms of slavery and death. . . . Let us always remember: the Lord is the Living One, he is merciful. The Lord is the Living One, he is merciful.

Ask for the Grace of Unity

Conflicts, if not properly resolved, divide us from each other, separate us from God. Conflict can help us to grow, but it can also divide us. Let us not go down the path of division, of fighting among ourselves! All united, all united in our differences, but united, always: this is the way of Jesus. Unity is superior to conflict. Unity is a grace for which we must ask the Lord, that he may liberate us from the temptation of division, of conflict between us, of selfishness, of gossip. How much evil gossip does, how much evil! Never gossip about others, never!

Do I Create Unity or Division?

We must all ask ourselves: how do I let myself be guided by the Holy Spirit in such a way that my life and witness of faith is both unity and communion? Do I convey the word of reconciliation and of love, which is the gospel, to the milieus in which I live? At times it seems that we are repeating today what happened at Babel: division, the incapacity to understand one another, rivalry, envy, egoism. What do I do with my life? Do I create unity around me? Or do I cause division, by gossip, criticism, or envy? What do I do? Let us think about this.

Passing from Slavery to Freedom

Christ died and rose once for all and for everyone, but the power of the resurrection, this passover from slavery to evil to the freedom of goodness, must be accomplished in every age, in our concrete existence, in our everyday lives. How many deserts, even today, do human beings need to cross! Above all, the desert within, when we have no love for God or neighbor, when we fail to realize that we are guardians of all that the Creator has given us and continues to give us. God's mercy can make even the driest land become a garden, can restore life to dry bones (cf. Ezekiel 37:1-14).

LIVING AS CHILDREN OF GOD

We Are Not Part-Time Christians

Let us ask ourselves . . . what steps we are taking to ensure that faith governs the whole of our existence. We are not Christian "part-time," only at certain moments, in certain circumstances, in certain decisions; no one can be Christian in this way. We are Christian all the time! Totally! May Christ's truth, which the Holy Spirit teaches us and gives to us, always and totally affect our daily life. Let us call on him more often so that he may guide us on the path of disciples of Christ. Let us call on him every day.

Bearing Fruit in the Real World

Christians are "spiritual." This does not mean that we are people who live "in the clouds," far removed from real life, as if it were some kind of mirage. No! The Christian is someone who thinks and acts in everyday life according to God's will, someone who allows his or her life to be guided and nourished by the Holy Spirit, to be a full life, a life worthy of true sons and daughters. And this entails realism and fruitfulness. Those who let themselves be led by the Holy Spirit are realists; they know how to survey and assess reality. They are also fruitful; their lives bring new life to birth all around them.

What It Means to Be Christian

Being Christian is not just obeying orders but means being in Christ, thinking like him, acting like him, loving like him; it means letting him take possession of our life and change it, transform it, and free it from the darkness of evil and sin.

Stake Your Lives on Noble Ideas

Commit yourselves to great ideals, to the most important things. We Christians were not chosen by the Lord for little things; push onwards toward the highest principles. Stake your lives on noble ideals.

Do We Act in Accordance with God?

When we say that a Christian is a spiritual being, we mean just this: the Christian is a person who thinks and acts in accordance with God, in accordance with the Holy Spirit. But I ask myself, and do we: do we think in accordance with God? Do we act in accordance with God? Or do we let ourselves be guided by the many other things that certainly do not come from God? Each one of us needs to respond to this in the depths of his or her own heart.

The Dignity of Children of God

Our filial relationship with God is not like a treasure that we keep in a corner of our life, but must be increased. It must be nourished every day with listening to the word of God, with prayer, with participation in the sacraments, especially Reconciliation and the Eucharist, and with love. We can live as children! And this is our dignity— we have the dignity of children. We should behave as true children! This means that every day we must let Christ transform us and conform us to him; it means striving to live as Christians, endeavoring to follow him in spite of seeing our limitations and weaknesses. The temptation to set God aside in order to put ourselves at the center is always at the door, and the experience of sin injures our Christian life, our being children of God.

Do Not Walk Alone

Walking is an art; if we are always in a hurry, we tire and cannot reach our destination, the destination of our journey. Yet if we stop and do not move, we also fail to reach our destination. Walking is precisely the art of looking to the horizon, thinking about where I want to go, and also coping with the weariness that comes from walking. Moreover, the way is often hard going; it is not easy. "I want to stay faithful to this journey, but it is not easy: listen, there is darkness; there are days of darkness, days of failure, and some days of falling . . . someone falls, falls." Yet always keep this in your thoughts: do not be afraid of failure, do not be afraid of falling. In the art of walking, it is not falling that matters, but not "staying fallen." Get up quickly, immediately, and continue to go on. . . . But also, it is terrible to walk alone, terrible and tedious. Walking in community, with friends, with those who love us: this helps us; it helps us to arrive precisely at the destination where we must arrive.

The Courage of Our Faith

We must have the courage of faith not to allow ourselves to be guided by the mentality that tells us, "God is not necessary, he is not important for you," and so forth. It is exactly the opposite: only by behaving as children of God, without despairing at our shortcomings, at our sins, only by feeling loved by him will our lives be new, enlivened by serenity and joy. God is our strength! God is our hope!

Work Fills Us with Dignity

The Book of Genesis tells us that God created man and woman, entrusting them with the task of filling the earth and subduing it, which does not mean exploiting it but nurturing and protecting it, caring for it through their work (cf. Genesis 1:28; 2:15). Work is part of God's loving plan; we are called to cultivate and care for all the goods of creation and, in this way, share in the work of creation! Work is fundamental to the dignity of a person. Work, to use a metaphor, "anoints" us with dignity, fills us with dignity, makes us similar to God, who has worked and still works, who always acts (cf. John 5:17). It gives one the ability to maintain oneself, one's family, to contribute to the growth of one's own nation.

A Heart Attentive to Jesus

We must be magnanimous, with a big heart, without fear, always betting on the great ideals. However, this also means magnanimity in little things, in daily things—the big heart, the great heart. And it is important to find this magnanimity with Jesus, in contemplating Jesus. Jesus is the One who opens windows for us on the horizon. Magnanimity means walking with Jesus, with a heart attentive to what Jesus tells us.

Politics: A Christian Duty

Involvement in politics is an obligation for a Christian. We Christians cannot "play the role of Pilate," washing our hands of it—we cannot. We must be involved in politics because politics is one of the highest forms of charity, for it seeks the common good. And Christian laypeople must work in politics. You will say to me, "But it isn't easy!" Nor is it easy to become a priest. Nothing is easy in life. It is not easy; politics has become too dirty, but I ask myself: why has it become dirty? Why aren't Christians involved in politics with an evangelical spirit? I leave you with a question. It is easy to say, "It is so-and-so's fault." But me, what do I do? It is a duty! Working for the common good is a Christian's duty! And often the way to work for that is politics. There are other ways: being a teacher, for example; teaching is another route. However, political life for the common good is one of the ways. This is clear.

Jesus Wants Us Free

Jesus does not want selfish Christians who follow their own ego, who do not talk to God. Nor does he want weak Christians, Christians who have no will of their own, "remote-controlled" Christians incapable of creativity, who always seek to connect with the will of someone else and are not free. Jesus wants us free. And where is this freedom created? It is created in dialogue with God in the person's own conscience. If a Christian is unable to speak with God, if he cannot hear God in his own conscience, he is not free; he is not free.

Conscience Means Listening to God

The conscience is the interior place for listening to the truth, to goodness, for listening to God; it is the inner place of my relationship with him, the One who speaks to my heart and helps me to discern, to understand the way I must take and, once the decision is made, to go forward, to stay faithful.

We have had a marvelous example of what this relationship with God is like, a recent and marvelous example. Pope Benedict XVI gave us this great example when the Lord made him understand, in prayer, what the step was that he had to take. With a great sense of discernment and courage, he followed his conscience, that is, the will of God speaking in his heart. And this example of our Father does such great good to us all, as an example to follow.

Without Grace We Can Do Nothing!

If I let myself be touched by the grace of the Risen Christ, if I let him change me in that aspect of mine which is not good, which can hurt me and others, I allow the victory of Christ to be affirmed in my life, to broaden its beneficial action. This is the power of grace! Without grace we can do nothing. Without grace we can do nothing! And with the grace of Baptism and of Eucharistic Communion, I can become an instrument of God's mercy, of that beautiful mercy of God.

SOURCES

Chapter 1: The Tender Love of God

1. God's Name Is Love: Angelus Address, St. Peter's Square, Solemnity of the Most Holy Trinity, May 26, 2013

2. The Cascade of Tenderness: Homily, St. Peter's Basilica, Mass with Seminarians, Novices, and Those Discerning Their Vocation, July 7, 2013

3. Faith in God's Tangible Love: *Lumen Fidei*, 17

4. We Are Not a Number to God: Homily, Basilica of St. John Lateran, Divine Mercy Sunday, April 7, 2013

5. God Takes the First Step: General Audience, St. Peter's Square, March 27, 2013

6. Like a Shepherd: General Audience, St. Peter's Square, March 27, 2013

7. God's Love: Stronger Than Death: Urbi et Orbi Message, Easter Sunday, March 31, 2013

8. God Is Patient with Us: Homily, Basilica of St. John Lateran, Divine Mercy Sunday, April 7, 2013

9. A Completely Reliable Love: *Lumen Fidei*, 17

Chapter 2: Encountering Jesus

7. Jesus Trusts in His Heavenly Father: Angelus Address, St. Peter's Square, June 2, 2013

8. What Is "the" Truth?: General Audience, St. Peter's Square, May 15, 2013

9. Christ Is Our Roped Guide: General Audience, St. Peter's Square, April 17, 2013

10. Present in Every Space and Time: General Audience, St. Peter's Square, April 17, 2013

11. The Heart of Jesus: Not Just a Symbol: Angelus Address, St. Peter's Square, June 9, 2013

12. He Makes Himself a Gift: Homily, Basilica of St. John Lateran, Solemnity of Corpus Christi, May 30, 2013

13. He Has Bent Down to Heal Us: Homily, St. Peter's Square, Palm Sunday, March 24, 2013

14. Seeing as Jesus Sees: *Lumen Fidei*, 18

15. Believing in Jesus: *Lumen Fidei*, 18

Chapter 3: Guided by the Spirit

10. The Gift of the Risen Christ: Homily, St. Peter's Square, Mass for *Evangelium Vitae* Day, June 16, 2013

Chapter 4: Trusting in God's Mercy

1. The Courage to Go to Jesus: Homily, Basilica of St. John Lateran, Divine Mercy Sunday, April 7, 2013

2. Don't Be Afraid of Your Weakness: Homily, Basilica of St. John Lateran, Divine Mercy Sunday, April 7, 2013

3. He Never Tires of Forgiving Us: Angelus Address, St. Peter's Square, March 17, 2013

4. God Always Thinks with Mercy: General Audience, St. Peter's Square, March 27, 2013

5. We Have an Advocate in Jesus: General Audience, St. Peter's Square, April 17, 2013

6. Jesus' Mercy Gives Life: Angelus Address, St. Peter's Square, June 9, 2013

7. God's Mercy Leads Us On: Homily, Basilica of St. John Lateran, Divine Mercy Sunday, April 7, 2013

8. The Lord's Most Powerful Message: Homily, Parish of St. Anna in the Vatican, March 17, 2013

Chapter 5: Proclaiming the Gospel

Chapter 6: Don't Forget the Poor

4. Touching the Flesh of Christ: Address, St. Peter's Square, Vigil of Pentecost with Ecclesial Movements, May 18, 2013

5. Poverty Demands That We Have Hope: Dialogue with Students of Jesuit Schools of Italy and Albania, Paul VI Audience Hall, June 7, 2013

6. The Real Crisis: Dialogue with Students of Jesuit Schools of Italy and Albania, Paul VI Audience Hall, June 7, 2013

7. The Sin of Indifference: Homily, Visit to Lampedusa, July 8, 2013

8. Has Anyone Wept in Our World Today?: Homily, Visit to Lampedusa, July 8, 2013

Chapter 7: Mother Mary, Help Us

1. Mary Shows Us How to Live in the Spirit: Regina Caeli Address, St. Peter's Square, April 28, 2013

2. She Always Hurries to Us: Homily to First Communicant Children, Roman Parish of Sts. Elizabeth and Zachariah, May 26, 2013

3. Mary's Example: Love God and Neighbor: Address at Meeting with the Missionaries of Charity at the Homeless Shelter *Dono di Maria*, May 21, 2013

Chapter 8: Gifts of Faith, Hope, and Joy

7. Our Hope Is Safe and Sound: General Audience, St. Peter's Square, April 10, 2013

8. The Joy of Being Children of God: General Audience, St. Peter's Square, April 10, 2013

9. Remember What God Has Done for You: Homily, St. Peter's Basilica, Easter Vigil, March 30, 2013

10. The Courage to Swim Against the Tide: St. Peter's Square, Mass and Conferral of the Sacrament of Confirmation, April 28, 2033

11. A Christian Can Never Be Sad: Homily, St. Peter's Square, Palm Sunday, March 24, 2013

12. The Resurrection Opens Us to Hope: General Audience, St. Peter's Square, April 3, 2013

Chapter 9: Pray Every Day

1. Give God Space in Prayer: General Audience, St. Peter's Square, May 1, 2013

2. Let the Lord Look at You: Address, St. Peter's Square, Vigil of Pentecost with Ecclesial Movements, May 18, 2013

Chapter 10: The Church Is Our Family

Chapter 11: Dealing with Trials and Temptations

1. God Grants Strength to Our Weakness: Homily, St. Peter's Square, Mass and Conferral of the Sacrament of Confirmation, April 28, 2013

2. God Can Change Any Situation: Homily, St. Peter's Basilica, Easter Vigil, March 30, 2013

3. Stripping Ourselves of Idols: Homily, Basilica of St. Paul Outside-the-Walls, April 14, 2013

4. Trials Lead to God's Glory: Homily, St. Peter's Square, Mass and Conferral of the Sacrament of Confirmation, April 28, 2013

5. Do Not Fear Commitment: Address, Recital of the Rosary, Basilica of St. Mary Major, May 4, 2013

6. Choose Life: Homily, St. Peter's Square, Mass for *Evangelium Vitae* Day, June 16, 2013

7. Ask for the Grace of Unity: General Audience, St. Peter's Square, June 19, 2013

8. Do I Create Unity or Division?: General Audience, St. Peter's Square, May 22, 2013

9. Passing from Slavery to Freedom: Urbi et Orbi Message, Easter Sunday, March 31, 2013

Chapter 12: Living as Children of God

1. We Are Not Part-Time Christians: General Audience, St. Peter's Square, May 15, 2013

2. Bearing Fruit in the Real World: Homily, St. Peter's Square, Mass for *Evangelium Vitae* Day, June 16, 2013

3. What It Means to Be Christian: General Audience, St. Peter's Square, April 10, 2013

4. Stake Your Lives on Noble Ideas: Homily, St. Peter's Square, Mass and Conferral of the Sacrament of Confirmation, April 28, 2013

5. Do We Act in Accordance with God?: General Audience, St. Peter's Square, May 8, 2013

6. The Dignity of Children of God: General Audience, St. Peter's Square, April 10, 2013

7. Do Not Walk Alone: Dialogue with Students of Jesuit Schools of Italy and Albania, Paul VI Audience Hall, June 7, 2013

8. The Courage of Our Faith: General Audience, St. Peter's Square, April 10, 2013

9. Work Fills Us with Dignity: General Audience, St. Peter's Square, May 1, 2013

10. A Heart Attentive to Jesus: Dialogue with Students of Jesuit Schools of Italy and Albania, Paul VI Audience Hall, June 7, 2013

11. Politics: A Christian Duty: Dialogue with Students of Jesuit Schools of Italy and Albania, Paul VI Audience Hall, June 7, 2013

12. Jesus Wants Us Free: Angelus Address, St. Peter's Square, June 30, 2013

13. Conscience Means Listening to God: Angelus Address, St. Peter's Square, June 30, 2013

14. Without Grace We Can Do Nothing!: Regina Caeli Address, St. Peter's Square, April 1, 2013